PRAISE FOR

"These marvelous poems offer the reader both invitation and gift—when you say yes, the treasures lay themselves out like a banquet for the heart. I love the sense of both longing and fullness held in tension through image and rhythm, a quiet knowing and wise unknowing revealed in the spaces between the words, and the grace of stillness beckoning from each poem."

—CHRISTINE VALTERS PAINTNER, poet, retreat leader, and author of *The Wisdom of the Body* and *Illuminating the Way: Embracing the Wisdom of Monks and Mystics*

"To read Mark S. Burrows' poems in *The Chance of Home* is to take a walk with the saints, both the churched and the literary, and to see the sun-struck wonder of the world 'here below' through their and his eyes. Burrows is the gracious poet-guide on our journey, teaching the wisdom of Rilke, Augustine, Simone Weil, Heraclitus, Emily Dickinson, and Jesus, singing the song of 'the lure of distances,' feeding us with 'crumbs . . . enough to make a feast,' and revealing to us at every turn the 'glimpse of home in the ordinary of it all.' For home is both where we are and where we are heading in these poems as they paint the world we are lucky enough to inhabit, luminous and lit from within, a universe of mute beautiful things that somehow sing through the poet's loving and attentive acts of translation and celebration. Burrows' poems are delicate tunes, brief epiphanies, faithful assurances against the uncertainties of eternity. It is a joy to march in step with his song, to stand surrounded by that cloud of witnesses, to be in that number."

—ANGELA ALAIMO O'DONNELL, poet, professor of English, Creative Writing and American Catholic Studies at Fordham University, and author of *Still Pilgrim: Poems* and *Lover's Almanac*

"It gives me great joy to read *The Chance of Home*: its gentle confidence fills me with hope. Often these poems put me into that serene Wordsworthian mood when I find I am 'become a living soul.' But they also confront silence, darkness and homelessness: in their evoking of song, they gather into themselves 'the most ancient of things,' understanding with Wallace Stevens that 'poetry is a part of the structure reality.' Mark S. Burrows' work beautifully manifests this truth as it provides a 'chance,' or song-filled sense, of home for the wandering soul on earth."

—EDWARD CLARKE, professor of English and creative writing at Oxford University, and author of *The Vagabond Spirit of Poetry* and *The Later Affluence of W.B. Yeats and Wallace Stevens*

"These wise and tender poems practice what Mark S. Burrows calls 'long listening,' a focused attentiveness to the particulars of skies, clouds, trees, geese and songbirds; to city streets and the homeless; to his wife, children and cats. Call these meditative poems Burrows' yes to the given world, his ongoing record of those instances of connectedness when we are at home in what Pessoa called 'the astonishing reality of things,' a reality which is, as Burrows so touchingly knows, 'nothing less than / the ordinary miracle of everything.'"

—ROBERT CORDING, poet and author of *Walking with Ruskin* and *Only So Far*

"Into this remarkable, grace-filled book of poems Mark S. Burrows has poured out his soul about the wisdom of place and the risks we must take to find and define it in the flow of life. For Burrows 'the chance of home' depends not simply on location but extends 'beyond maps' into the 'vast geography of grace.' The central question these powerful poems address is this: How do we belong? *The Chance for Home* thus reflects Burrows' journey as the survivor of the 'grit of loss [and] the grind of grief' as well as his witness to the epiphanies experienced along the way. So many of these are beautifully expressed, almost Wordsworthian, in his poems about nature—crocuses 'spear[ing] their greening blades / up beyond the hold of winter's grip,' the wisdom of trees with their 'seasoned play,' the 'gift of cloud and wind and dreaming mind,' and a swaying line of geese that 'carves a wedge through the empty acres of the sky.' *The Chance of Home* offers the courage we need to accept a wisdom that 'lures us by what we long for, and [finds] us within the reach of what we seek.' With his beautiful book Burrows has established himself as a major poet of fortitude and faith."

—PHILIP C. KOLIN, editor of *The Southern Quarterly*, and author of *Benedict's Daughter* and *Emmett Till in Different States*

"This collection gathers us again to wonder at what has been given to us every day, anywhere. Mark S. Burrows' poems invite us to see more than we see, beckoning us to wonder and to marvel. Rilke is listening here, and Wallace Stevens, too, but the distinctive voice is Burrows' own music, at once sensuous and full of Augustinian, even apophatic, longing."

—DON SALIERS, theologian, Emory University, coauthor of *A Song to Sing, a Life to Live*, and author of *Music and Theology*

"In these elegant poems of stately simplicity and lyrical rhythms, Mark S. Burrows crafts a poetry that is resonant with what is reverential, as in 'the poplar that girds the road's far bend.' This is a poetry that exhibits the conjuring of sacred image, 'like a word that breathes unheard in / what we know but can never fully say.' These poems often give expression to a stony Thomas Merton-like inner well of solitude. They reflect, as in the poem 'Cloudwatch,' a 'dreaming mind' through which we experience 'glimpses of enduring things that gather / us in the radiance of this passing world.' This is a book of essences, whose author is drawn by the seasonal migrations of geese. Like those flocks, these poems consistently point to the true north on life's metaphysical compass; they offer the reader 'what we / need to brave the stinging cold.' Ultimately, however, this is a poetry of praise, which opens from within its own center, as does the lily."

—WALLY SWIST, poet and author of *Huang Po and the Dimensions of Love* and, with David Breeden and Steven Schroeder, *Daodejing*.

The Chance of Home

The Chance of Home

Mark S. Burrows

Poems

✝
PARACLETE PRESS
BREWSTER, MASSACHUSETTS

2018 First Printing

The Chance of Home

Copyright © 2018 by Mark S. Burrows

ISBN 978-1-61261-647-6

Library of Congress Cataloging-in-Publication Data

Names: Burrows, Mark S., 1955- author.
Title: The chance of home : poems / Mark S. Burrows.
Description: Brewster MA : Paraclete Press Inc., [2017]
Identifiers: LCCN 2016048997 | ISBN 9781612616476 (softcover)
Classification: LCC PS3602.U76875 A6 2017 | DDC 811/.6--dc23
LC record available at https://lccn.loc.gov/2016048997

10 9 8 7 6 5 4 3 2 1

Published by Paraclete Press
Brewster, Massachusetts
www.paracletepress.com

Printed in the United States of America

For my daughters
Emma and Madeline

with gratitude for their love,
"with its vast geography of grace"

Learn what your body / Your boundary, teaches you.
—FERNANDO PESSOA

My question was the attention I gave to the things around me,
and their answer was their beauty.
—AUGUSTINE OF HIPPO

Beauty is the only finality here below.
—SIMONE WEIL

CONTENTS

This Long Listening

As True As Song

An Everlasting Yes

Entrance

Whoever you are, as evening falls leave
your little room where you know everything,
for your house stands on the verge of distances,
whoever you are.
With eyes so tired they can barely
lift themselves from the worn-out sill,
raise with measured gaze a single black tree
and place it before the skies, slender and alone.
And you've made the world. And it is vast,
and like a word still ripening in the silences.
And just as your will grasps its meaning,
your eyes tenderly let it go . . .

—RAINER MARIA RILKE

TRANSLATED BY MARK S. BURROWS

This Long Listening

There is a story of a religious teacher who used to talk every morning to his disciples. One morning he got on to the platform and was just about to begin when a little bird came and sat on the window sill and begin to sing, and sang away with full heart. Then it stopped and flew away and the teacher said, "The sermon for this morning is over."

—KRISHNAMURTI

I Still Marvel

Each spring I wait for the crocuses to come,
eager to greet their purple bursts as they rise

from the soggy earth and stubborn patches
of late-lingering snow, and while I know

what their veils will show of radiance,
this does nothing to blunt my wonder

at their shining spread across the lawn.
They never bother to argue or complain,

but simply spear their greening blades
up beyond the hold of winter's grip,

as if to sing in a gentle soundless way.
And though I've seen all this before,

I still marvel when they come, stem and
leaf and flower unfurling themselves

from the clutch of roots, a patience we
yearn for, a lure of this long listening.

FIRST LISTENING

*Animals and physical matter find a voice through those
who contemplate them.*
—*Augustine of Hippo*

When the rains fall after a long
drought as they did last night,

you can almost hear the bursts
of laughter and sense the ease

of the gnarly old olive trees,
breaking the watchful silences

they've kept among themselves.
And while we think it's ours to

give them voice, it could be
they're the ones first listening.

THE STILLNESS OF THINGS

Something deep within us yearns for
the stillness of things that cannot speak—

stones raised in a fresh-ploughed field or
the poplar that girds the road's far bend,

the spread of poppies swaying in morning
winds or waves astir on a blue-shining sea.

All these bear witness in ways we can't
quite hear but somehow sense, like a hymn

whose unstrung rhymes carry us through
the long hours, or a solitude that sings

within the restless fling of flowing time,
like a word that breathes unheard in what

we vaguely know but can never fully say.

A Late-Summer Breakfast in a Mountain Ash

All morning long she serves hunger's call,
this thrush who moves carefully from branch

to branch as she plucks her way through
the clumps of orange fruit, emptying

the tree of its harvest; in this she's drawn
not by appetite alone but by the stubborn

habits of desire, knowing she must feast
before turning south again away from

winter's hold, like the heart whose
yearning bounds the absences.

A FEW OF THE PARTICULARS

The harmony past knowing sounds more deeply
than the known.
　　　　—Heraclitus

I make my way listening among the hours and the days,
attending to a few of the particulars: the chatter of a finch

hidden in the foliage; the laughter of a child from behind
a sheltering hedge; the swirling autumn winds rustling

the last brittle leaves that still cling to the old oak's arms,
long practiced in the art of holding up the acres of sky.

Each opens our eyes to the ever-forward fling of things;
each gestures to a deeper flow than we can ever know or

finally say. Among these I look for traces of a hidden
whole, gazing on what I cannot grasp within the glimpse

of what I can, opening my breath to the lure of distances
that pulses in all that lives in this theater of here and now.

No Permanence

The dune grasses have no language of their own,
gesturing in murmurs we can almost overhear.

They seem to whisper on calmer days but then
wake to louder ways when the winds rise to twist

them where they stand and coax from them an
almost soundless song. So, too, the shifting sands

that hold them with their loosely rooted feet;
they know no permanence of form but wander

on, and as they do they carry the dunes along as
they make their way along the edges of the sea,

reminding us that we live amid the changes, a part
of an unseen whole that ever flows and never stays,

like wind and wave that drift without beginning or
end and seem to dance in their mostly silent ways.

In Dry Times

This morning a gentle wind stirs the spread of brittle leaves
that lie like a crumpled carpet beneath this stand of olive trees.

Some have stood for centuries, and I wonder as I walk among
them who labored here and what they knew of gladness or grief.

At grove's edge an abandoned threshing floor opens a circle to
the sun, inlaid with stones worn smooth by wind and use and rain;

beyond this sits a tidy row of beehives, and as I come near I hear
the whir of their wings, darting about among the rows of flowers

that weight these boughs in spring, while in late-summer days they
will have to search far and wide to taste the sweetness they crave.

They trust that desire will carry them far and then back home
across the distances, like trust when all reason for it is gone or

hope that holds us against the heart's drought, that lures us by
what we long for and finds us within the reach of what we seek.

A Single Thirst

Today the rain falls in dark sheets driven
by gravity and wind, and all the while

a flock of white-throated sparrows nestles
snugly beneath a scraggly rosemary bush,

seeking what shelter they can find, each
joined in a single thirst, wing and twig alike

bound in unintended praise. They know no
other way than this against the biting cold,

staying close to share the little warmth they
have as if in promise of an enduring end.

THE CERTAINTIES OF PLACE

The trees keep a vigil in obedience
to gravity and the certainties of place.

They imagine no journey, no going
forth at all, yet each calls silently

to those who walk idly among them
in the wisdom of their seasoned play.

They don't reason as we do, but in
their listening might well wonder

what it is that presses us so and
keeps us still in our hurried pace.

The Waiting Wonders

If I speak of Nature, it's not because I know what it is
But because I love it.
           —*Fernando Pessoa*

The door of morning opens gently each day,
not demanding a thing of us but hoping

we'll have eyes to catch some measure of
the waiting wonders and their delights—

like the glistening jewels gathered at
the tips of the spruce's glistening arms,

left behind by rains that pounded all
night long, or the buzz of hummingbirds

who've come searching for honeyed gold
hidden in the peonies' soft uncurling heads,

while a flock of clouds wanders slowly out
across the wide blue meadows of the sky.

All these are only what they are, and yet
they offer us glimpses of a gift stronger

than our longest losses and deeper than
what we know of sorrow and grief, glances

of the shining that still might save us who
know to listen, lingering, and to gaze.

COPLEY SQUARE

—in grateful memory of Harry Huff, who loved all this

It is not a square like those of old Europe,
ringed with small cafes where the men spend
their days drinking strong coffee and talk on
and on in this slow liturgy of the hours.

Absent here the relentless burn of the sun,
the whine of mopeds grinding hard against
what the day knows of song, the bright colors
that once blazed ancient stuccoed walls, now

washed away by seasons of rain and neglect,
the banter of their talk an ebb and flow like
the tides that come and go, rising and falling
against the long intractable ledges of time.

THE LONG CALL HOME

As the days grow cold, I watch the geese
as they heed the lure of warmer shores;

they announce themselves from afar,
and then they're suddenly upon us,

drifting high overhead as their swaying
line carves a wedge through the empty

acres of the sky. Sometimes they turn
suddenly east or west or north again,

searching for what they need to endure
this flight; they'll follow a way that

leads them far from here and then back
again, drawn by the longing that lures

them to greet the returning surge of
warmth. But now my eyes follow them

as they pass over and by, reminding me of
what I also know of the long call home.

The Enduring Things

We do not obtain the most precious gifts by going
in search of them but by waiting for them.
—*Simone Weil*

The enduring things find us when we wait
for them, taking their shape in the places of

fear and the silent murmurings of despair,
but when we bid them stay and dare to sing

them into some whispered song they're often
gone before they've ever fully come, leaving

faint traces behind where we must wait—
like April's gestures toward a coming May,

or memories of one taken by an early grave,
like a dream that faintly echoes your name.

WHAT HERE ABIDES

Perhaps something suddenly will happen
and pulse with hidden truth.
—Anna Kamieńska

Outside my window, the late light
glazes the last stubborn oak leaves,

always somehow reluctant to let go,
their brittle brown mantle defying

the winds before they once more fall
back to earth again. Week by week

they outwait the more vibrant dress
of other trees, throwing dappled

shadows on what lies beneath them
of farm and field and the figure of

an old woman walking slowly down
the worn path, bent low by the press

of years and burdens I cannot know.
All the while a single hawk circles

high above, his wings flashing in
the late-day sun, riding the updrafts

in long loops across the sky as he
looks intently for what moves below.

And as I watch I see traces of what
shines in all this, beginning to let go

of my need to know what any of it
might mean, and take my place in

the family of things—a glimpse
of beauty caught within this flow,

a simple sort of praise, a sense of
now and what here abides of home.

The Hungering Dark

What happens when we measure silence and say that a
given period of silence lasted as long as a given sound?
—*Augustine of Hippo*

A lone goose drifts out across
the empty crease of sky above

stubbled fields below, not
heeding the flock's broken line,

steering her course alone into
the pooling magnitudes of night.

From where I walk I listen to her
cry as she passes high above

and singly by, and wait but hear
no answer to her fervent call.

Minutes pass as she pleads
her case over and over against

the crease of death, a reminder
of a gift once given and taken

back again, a call that drifts on
and on into the hungering dark.

Turnings Like These

> *But yet I know, where'er I go,*
> *That there hath pass'd away a glory from the earth.*
> —William Wordsworth

This year the first snow fell in September,
riding a blast of cold just as we'd gotten

used to the golden sun-splashed days of fall.
Under the weight of this heavy blanket no

sound can be heard save the muffled stir
of voices drifting somewhere out of sight.

Nothing can hold the seasons' flight or stay
these feelings when they come; like winter's

call with pounding northern winds, this turn
reminds us of absences we must also face,

like silences that settle when the last lines
of birdsong yield to the hushing lull of night,

the rustle of late-autumn leaves that soon
enough will fall, like the stillness that settles

over us as darkness descends on branch
and bridge and hedge and house. I've faced

all this many times before, and will again,
intimations of mortality with its gains before

the stubborn losses that will surely come.

THE WISDOM OF PLACE

The trees stand still where they
first set roots, never doubting

the wisdom of place, refusing
the empty strain and race of time.

Loss they know but not, with us,
the growing old and letting go,

and though their thin green dress
flutters now like shining sails in

a summer breeze, soon enough
they'll greet the waiting glaze

of golds and burnished oranges
and reds that come to blaze

the day's blue September face.
But first they'll tremble one last

time, then loose their grip and
yield to a stillness that holds all

this and us with a vibrant grace—
their final call to sing before they

fall back toward those who linger
among them, listening, below.

CLOUDWATCH

Things tell us through stories what they don't say.
    —*Fernando Pessoa*

The clouds drift aimlessly by, free
of worry and the doubts that nag us so;
they make their way far out across

the bluing heights that play above
the gathering uncertainties below,
strutting in their changing forms as

they come and go. In all this they're
so unlike us, shifting shape easily—
from dog to dragon to elephant

as we watch, then suddenly a rabbit
with ears atilt as if listening for sounds
we might still know or learn to make.

On this late-summer day I lie lazily
in the grass with my dreaming daughter
of six, sprawled out in a meadow that

stretches down to the sea, and join her
in this cloudwatch. She gazes, and as
she starts to name what she finds, I, too,

begin to see them: *Look, Dad,* she cries,
a horse! and there—a fairy! and slowly I
begin to take this world of wonders in,

21

this drifting realm of forms that meets
our playful eyes—as a lone mare saunters
above us and gladly by, all of this a gift

of cloud and wind and dreaming mind,
all glimpses of enduring things that gather
us in the radiance of this passing world.

The Evidence of Things Not Seen

*To reach for something else than the facts will
carry you beyond [the city without desire], and
perhaps, as with Socrates, beyond this world.*
—Anne Carson

We're made for this: to reach beyond what we
dimly see or hope to grasp, stretching our minds
toward what may be an emptiness without return—

or more. And so when darkness settled against tides
of unrelenting desire, I found myself facing the dull
crease of death with its undertow of loss and pain;

listening now to the silences that linger long after
the last stirrings have settled in the empty house,
I wonder what it will be like to tend the fire alone

whose embers have faded against the pressing cold,
and mend through the long days and longer nights,
and if I'll dare to cross the threshold of love again.

Three Silences

One silence carves away
slowly into an ancient stone ledge,
drop by falling drop,

an ecstasy only
for those who know the endurances
of change.

A second stalks us
amid the wars we tolerate and make,
the violence

chiseled hard into
the bodies of those who face a shock
they'll never know as awe.

On the evening news,
an old woman bent over by age and care
tends a single flower

that rises from
the parched earth; with one trembling hand
she clutches

an old watering can,
with the other, a yellowed photograph of
her lost son.

Hers is another
silence, a grave resistance against
the madness.

THE LURE OF DISTANCES

A line of geese heads north across
the broad belt of sky, steering far out

beyond any boundaries we can see.
They heed the lure of distances that

calls them in the caverns of desire,
an instinct shaped beyond what we

can listen for or ever finally hear.
Their habit seeks an end as far as

the heart can reach and farther
than the eye, their hunger drawn

by a longing with unfurled wings
that still somehow still know to fly.

THE ORDINARY OF IT ALL

*—a gentle sunrise over the Sierra Nevada mountains
at Hacienda Los Olivos, near Granada*

The way morning strokes the heavens
with her soft caress, her fingers reaching

into the long hollow of the night, covering
the darkness with the first shy crease of day,

and how hidden birds chatter on unseen,
their song stirring the stillnesses before

the first winds rise; the sight of my breath
curling in wisps as it meets the cool air,

and the silence of an enduring stand of
olive trees, so ancient and unmoving in

their ways, yet knowing how to raise
a harvest after long durations of thirst:

all these are more than what they seem,
each opening us to glimpses of home

held in the ordinary of it all, each one
a beckoning to linger and to praise.

Awaiting Prayer

—3:15 a.m., before Vigils at the Abbey of Gethsemane
(Trappist, Kentucky)

A single flame
pierces the
hold of night
that keeps the
old church,
its naked ribs
bracing
the roof,
my breath,
the silence
that shows
no interest
in my
questions,
the darkness
awaiting
prayer,
without
regard to
argument or
opinion—
not mine,
not any.

Beneath Our Speech

> *Silence contains everything within itself. It is not waiting for anything.*
> —Max Picard

A sign on each table in the abbey guesthouse
dining room reads: *Silence is spoken here,* and
so at dinner we gesture wordlessly after salt or
signal with our hands for more water or bread.

Hour by hour we settle into the comfort of this
unfamiliar discipline, an island in the sea of talk
from which we'd come, a silent refuge in this
word-drenched world that is too much with us.

Day by day the stillness roots in us more deeply,
at first a hum in the mind, and then with time
the place for a truer listening, a quiet call of
all that lives and breathes beneath our speech.

Like the Lion

Another November day heavy with clouds and
long on drizzling rain, the hours untouched by

reveries that sometimes come to startle us in
the length of a lazy mid-August haze; poems

often come like this, enlisting us for a song
we hardly knew when we began, stirring us

as if to call all our certainties into question.
When they come they demand nothing of us

and rarely fuss; they simply wait like the lion
whose prey does not yet sense the gravity of

the danger. For we're not here to wonder what
the waiting page means, or if the right words

will come, or if we who're stalked by poetry
are worthy of art's appetites. Like the lion.

Never still the question

that tumbles on and on unseen
beneath the surfaces of things,

the rhythm of daily tasks and
ordinary duties that lie like

the massive stones held still in
the river's depths, and shift

the pattern of the onward flow,
moving—if at all—only when

the pull is finally great enough
or the bottom gives way.

Perhaps for Love

Amor ubique loquitur.
        —*Bernard of Clairvaux (d. 1153)*

A friend writes to tell me of her work,
which is the call to make art with things

close to hand—bits of wood and clay and
odds and ends of what she makes or finds,

all gathered in the caverns of the heart.
And while I read her letter, although I

should be turned to other tasks, a poem
begins to woo me, despite the press of

things, and again I bow to the lilies' call—
not the ones tamed in the tidy shop, but

those that spread promiscuously along
the edges of the field, and all the while

the aroma of a curried-leek soup fills
the house, drifting from room to room

as if to defy Plato's claim that beauty
rests in eternal forms beyond this world.

And as I gaze across the fresh-mown
grass, a flock of clouds drifts out across

the noonday skies, living out the changes
without worry or shame, knowing as they

seem to do that *love speaks everywhere.*
Watching them, I begin to see what it

means to give myself to the winds and
their solace, to lie down beneath the trees

whose shadows play a constant game of
hide and seek, while on and on my cats

lie sleeping idly in the sun, their bodies
curled around each other for company

and for warmth, perhaps for love—
who can ever say?

What Lingers

We're always hurrying.
But this march of time—
it's of little worth among
what ever abides.

All that hastens
will soon be gone,
for what lingers
beyond initiates us.

Children, don't waste
your courage on speed
or squander it in flight.

All is at rest:
darkness and bright,
blossom and book.

—RAINER MARIA RILKE

TRANSLATED BY MARK S. BURROWS

As True as Song

Maybe there's a land where you have to sing to explain anything . . .

—WILLIAM STAFFORD

FRAGMENTS

I dwell in Possibility – / A fairer House than Prose –
    —Emily Dickinson

Last night in a dream I caught a glimpse of radiance
shining in the web of ordinary things—a snatch of talk

in a language I'd never heard but could just understand;
a sudden flare of light on a lake so remote I saw it only

from distances far above; and a room empty but for three
old armchairs, each worn from long use and well loved.

It wasn't like memory exactly, though it seemed to me
that these things were rising from some place of having

been already known. And though I'm sure I'd never
seen any of this before, it has become as much a part

of my life as the remembrance of things past, fragments
of experiences receding into the long keep of time,

all of it falling into losses and gains as true as song.

Call and Response

It is desire that saves.
—Simone Weil

I

What does the squirrel know of desire,
or the bee? And what of the bird?

Not the generic bird, since desire,
like birds, is never general, but

depends on the singularity of things
with their appetites and delights—

as with the unseen cuckoo I once
heard singing from somewhere deep

in the woods, her music reaching out
from the forest into wide fields where

I found myself walking toward dusk;
she never wonders if she should sing,

or for how long, calling into distances
with her persistent melancholic song.

II

Somewhere, not far, her mate answers
in bright peals of an echoing refrain,

his call drawn by the heart's hungers
where music finds its true shape, and

as he does he presses a shaft of breath
through the slender vessel of his throat,

his feathered body trembling, his call
spilling out into the wilderness of night.

And as I listen to this antiphony I start
to feel myself saved, at least a little,

from the burden of my importance,
lured by love's desire and by her song.

WHAT WE'RE MADE FOR

Song opposes the power of distance.
—*Jean-Louis Chrétien*

There are at least three reasons to sing:
because we can, sometimes because we

must, and yes, because in the deep-down
truth at the heart of things, silence does

not deserve the last word, because after
all is said and done we're not made for

the clarities of prose alone, but for what
song can bring of solace and delight.

Elementary Music

It was the fourth grade, and I knew it was the start
of a musical career, proud of my shiny clarinet rented
against the likely chance that the gift might not take.

After a few weeks I was able to make squawking
shrieks that no one would have thought to call music,
sounding more like an animal in some terrible agony,

with moments of metal grating on slate. And then it
came: the day of our first concert, our parents assembled
on the hard wooden bleachers of the grade school gym,

seeming undisturbed by it all, beaming with a pride
not yet chastened by the noise that soon enough would
be unleashed. The first piece began with a blast and off

we galloped, trying to translate into something like song
what we could just make out of the notes neatly scribed
on the page, and then it all fell apart as quickly as it had

begun, and we sat in nervous silence before the director
who paid no heed to our boisterous failure, standing
alert and ready, a look of pure anticipation on his face,

signaling us to attention as he raised his plastic baton
and then struck it several times against the music stand,
and off we raced again, like hounds chasing their prey

across soggy fields and out over stubborn thorny hedges,
making a sound that had never been heard before or since.
And after a frolic of reckless joy we all somehow sensed

that it was time to stop, our faces shining with the joy of
those who'd found some lost or deeply hidden treasure,
waiting for the applause we knew would surely come.

THAT EMPTY PLACE

—for Emma and Madeline, always

Outside the old gabled house
a lone warbler sings her heart into

this world with an unyielding joy;
she doesn't ask for more or fear

less than she has, her stage a branch
high up in the outstretched arms

of the old spruce beside our house.
From there she sounds her creed

without regard for any audience,
knowing nothing of tomorrow or

any other imagined thing; she sings
what she knows of love with its

vast geography of grace, filling with
her song that empty place within

where hope still waits to find us.

So, Too, the Heart

The old temple bell
still sings in the silences,
waiting for the hammer
to bring it again to song.

SACRAMENT OF SONG

—an Adelaide morning, in fond memory of Betty Smith,
lover of magpies and poems and other saving delights

Where do poems come from, and why so often mornings?
I don't ever know for sure, but I've got some hunches:

sometimes they rise from the drifting wake of dreams
that lead us through the haze of sleep, and at others

fall in bursts of reverie like the laughter I swear I once
overheard as I stood in a grove of ancient gum trees

shining after the dust of months of drought was washed
away by a downpour of rain, and sometimes they come

mimicking the magpies who consecrate each day with
their raucous sacrament of song. Whenever they come

it's best to welcome them without argument, avoiding
the gallop of unneeded syllables or heavy thoughts,

yielding to what they give us to see. And it's still just
possible that the magpies, despite their noisy chatter,

know more about all this than we do or ever will.

DESPITE THE ODDS

—for my brother John, and the ICU staff at Beth Israel/
Deaconess Medical Center, Boston

Among buildings devoted to the useful arts,
one seems to hold a special place, standing

as a mansion of care where nurses bear their
work with a tenderness they did not first

learn in school, where sirens sound amid the
endless din of city noise their groan of warning

or of wordless prayer. And still the tears of all
who come seeking some balm of healing here,

arriving heavy with anxiety or laden with fear,
call on something more precious than skill alone.

And still the heart sings on, despite the odds,
for hope is what we never finally learn to forget.

Knowing Nothing

I have with me / all that I do not know / I have lost none of it
—W. S. Merwin

Already at sunrise the birds are
busy at their work of praise,
knowing nothing of our neglect,
because there's music to be made
and song refuses to wait for some
proper occasion or place. In this
they're not like us who seldom sing,
steering the little bark of our lives
back from the deep into shallows
where music has but little reach.

Yet beauty still can have its way
with us and sometimes does,
luring us early and late with
the voice of the lark who never
hesitates to spill her joy out into
the wide acres of silence, shaping
in the hollow of her throat beams
of a kind of light that knows no end.
She sings her assent in cascading
peals and galloping trills, wooing
us with the radiance of her art
and the shining lure of song.

Whether or Not

The astonishing reality of things
Is my discovery every day.
—Fernando Pessoa

All along the days I listen
for them, these feathered

carriers of song. They don't
know why they sing, and

when they do don't think
about who, if anyone, might

be listening. Beauty is their
way, as stillness is for stone

and fragrance for the rose,
all of this a wonder whether

or not we notice it or give it
a name, whether or not it

raises us to sing, whether
or not it opens our heart

to wonder or to praise.

THE MASS. AVENUE BLUES

What had he been like as a child, I wonder,
this lonely homeless man who sits in an old
wheelchair in front of Citizens Bank, reigning
like the uncrowned King of Central Square?

He always has a harmonica tucked into his
front shirt pocket, pulling it out for any
who linger long enough to hear him sing—
The Mass Aaaaav'nue Bluuuuues, he begins,

I knows 'em well, I do. And then on he plays,
this man with time to spare, with stories to tell
and songs to make. Some days I walk on by,
but when I stop to ask him how he is, his eyes

meet mine each time with startled wonderment,
surprised when I greet him by name: *G'mornin'
Tom*, or *Harmonica T*, as he prefers to be called;
he's always glad to play his one mournful song,

slow and blue and long, and I become his audience
of one over the grind of cars and buses driving by
and the rumble of the Red Line trains below, and
when he's done, he looks me over with moist eyes

and begins to repeat slowly, as if for the first time,
the substance of his simple creed: *I jus' keeps on
playin' 'em, man, cuz the bluuuues, they keeps on
playin' us, oooh yes, you got to know they do."*

An Ode to Lavender and Mint

For I am the size of what I see...
—Fernando Pessoa

The flowers we plant in the spring together
with the volunteers that come of their own all

bloom indifferently, as with the lavender I
seeded in our garden together with the mint

that started in one spot and then wandered
off to visit its neighbors where they rooted.

In their obedient ways the first lifts tendrils
with soft sprays of purple flowers that promise

a coming yield of fragrance, while all along
the garden's edge the mischievous mint bears

aloft a spread of soft blue buds, both drawing
a constant buzzing pulse of bees. In this they

do just what they were meant to do, and no
more; their joy is this fragrant and free.

Magpie Praise

A song held is not a song at all,
wanting only to live by giving

itself away. And so it sails its
gentle soul out against the tides

of hesitation and despair, steering
through these currents in a little

bark made of music and delight.
The magpie knows this well

despite her noisy sort of praise,
which after all is a source of

art and the heart of what we
know of joy. Song rises from

the soft hollow of her breast
without arguing about style or

pace, and she never pauses to
ask if some nobler music might

be better, the cackle of her voice
a showy sort of prayer—a dazzle

of sound, a shaking of delight,
a deep and unrelenting mirth.

Her laughter lifts us into sheer
frivolity beyond the burdens we

must bear, a beam of light that
trembles as it rises from the night.

A Stubborn Parable

I don't know what Nature is: I sing it.
—*Fernando Pessoa*

This morning, sitting in a small enclosed garden,
I noticed a sprig of green clinging improbably to

a dark stone wall, its roots rising from a slender
crease where a stray seed once fell, carried by

the winds, perhaps, or some wayward bird—who
could ever tell? It somehow found an edge of soil

and held out against the thrust of winter's snow
and ice, lifting itself up toward the sun against

an unforgiving face of stone—a parable of grit,
the resilience of song, a strong resonance of hope.

AMONG THE UNCERTAINTIES

*What was scattered / gathers. / What was gathered /
blows apart.*
   —Heraclitus

The sun rises to meet us each day
for no reason we can ever explain,

casting long shadows that remain
indifferent to the clutter and clutch

of our minds, holding onto things
that soon enough are gone without

any reason we can know. None of
this is tragedy or chance, nor is it

a way to stay the time as it spills
on amid the uncertainties we face,

and all we make and we ourselves
rise only to fall at the last, despite

our strongest belief in permanence;
at our best we yield to the forward

flow of things as the winds do, stirring
song into the stillnesses without any

intent to teach and with a gladness
deeper than words can ever reach.

   —remembering September 11, after fifteen years

SOMETHING OF THE MERCY

Just after dawn I found the gentle dove
who'd sung so tenderly each morning

with what had seemed to me a grace of
exceeding sense. Her song was the work

she had to do, and she'd spilled it gladly into
the silences that lingered from the night.

Her voice was her gift, but this morning
stillness is all I heard, and when I went out

listening for her found her lying stiff and
cold, the little quiver of her breast split wide

to bare the hollow that had held her heart
and pumped the breath her song required,

and the first blaze of sun had already set
a dull glaze in her once darkly shining eyes.

I lifted her carefully with the spade of an old
shovel I'd fetched from the shed and placed

her in a shallow grave I'd dug in a corner
shaded by hyssop and bluestem and lavender,

sensing something of the mercy that will
one day gather us with her, too, in the way

that leads inevitably home.

A Longer Silence

The meadow grasses stand silently,
gesturing with unworded tongue;

theirs is a song inaudible to our ears,
a joy that rhymes unheard on quieter

days, a rhythm shaped by a pattern
made by their swirling blades on

blustery wind-swept days. The earth
that roots them keeps a longer silence

than theirs, standing its ground against
the durations of pounding winds and

driving rains. And all the while these
grasses breathe on and on amid what

ever changes, whispering their simple
part in the unfixed song of eternity.

In Answer

*The part of art which is art, and not device, unshackles us
from usefulness almost entirely.*
—Jane Hirshfield

A black-capped chickadee sings
hidden somewhere just out of sight,

her bursts of song filling silences
that linger from the deep of night.

Her music rises like a bright thread
of light woven of the gentle fabric

of sleep; she doesn't wait for eye
to see or ear to hear, but offers her

call without regard for audience.
Her music points beyond every

notion of purpose we can know,
in answer to the rising of the day

and the sometime coming of delight.

SAUDADE IN THE LISBON SUBWAY

To be great, be whole: don't exaggerate
Or leave out any part of you.
Be complete in each thing. Put all you are
Into the least of your acts.
  —Fernando Pessoa

Each day he works the Blue Line subway cars,
making his way slowly down the center aisle,

this wiry blind man in new jeans who carries
a bright steel pole with which he raps the floor,

tapping its side rhythmically with a metal stick;
a tin cup hangs around his neck on a silver chain

to gather gifts of change, and he sometimes beats
it like a cymbal as if to hold the shape of song.

He voices all this between the stops as he shuffles
among us, his head held high as he gives himself

to the calling of his art; when someone tosses a
coin in he turns as if to search for their face,

staring carefully with long-blank eyes, and then
sings on in lyric cadences of Portuguese, voicing

his thanks, perhaps, or shaping the start of a poem—
the next great Pessoa, who can say? He speaks

courteously to each, as one who serves, but reigns
as poets do in the dignities of rhythm and of rhyme.

What Glory

Consider the birds of the air . . . and the lilies of the field . . .
—*Jesus of Nazareth*

I

A lone sparrow sings into
the edging morning light,
spilling her praise into the

rising day. This is courage,
not to ask if the song is right,
repeating over and over in

short bursts—*cheep, cheep,*
chirrup. She never thinks of
some longer view but sings on

because she's made for this,
her body a feathered muscle
of praise which trills out

a clear and unrelenting *yes*;
her song is prayer unceasing,
a rhyme untouched by reason.

II

And what of the lilies?
We give them names—
Tinkerbell and Turk's Cap,

Trout and Trillium—all
witnesses without toil or
trade to what we try so

hard to grasp, their roots
lifting color from the fall
of light and deep of earth.

And what of us who sow
our endless seeds of worry
and persistent doubt?

What are we with
our most fervent cares
and earnest deeds?

What glory of ours
exceeds birdsong
or seedburst?

At All Times

*Attention animated by desire is the whole foundation of
religious practices.*
—*Simone Weil*

At vigils, one of the novices stumbles over a line from the psalms,
covers her mouth with shame and prostrates herself on the floor.

No one seems troubled by her mistake, and we simply wait for
the prayer to continue as it does when another sister takes up

where she had broken off. All this is so unlike the doves who
keep their watch outside the church, cooing quietly where they sit;

they're still at it when we finish, nuzzling each other against
the morning chill, undisturbed by us, knowing nothing of what

keeps us singing as we chant our way through the list of psalms,
while on and on they keep a promise without the force of vows:

"I shall bless the Lord at all times; his praise will ever be on my lips."
When our work is done we leave the church and walk over

to the dining room, joining the humbled sister for breakfast,
giving ourselves to the day's silences and the burdens that wait;

and still the doves sing on, knowing nothing of duty or of shame,
not needing any scriptural admonition to pray without ceasing.

STILL THE HEART

—with thanks to Wallace Stevens for the opening line and a half

It's not every day that the world arranges
itself in a poem, though some days it does,

a redbird singing brightly from somewhere
in the last creases of the night as the sun

braids her cords through the maple's arms,
still hidden in the veil of early-edging gold.

This is prayer, whether the mind agrees or
the ear attends, whether the bird has a name

or a tree. Most days, though, it's a world
of creatures and things keeping their own

counsel, the days and nights cycling by
without any purpose we can ever tell.

And all the while the redbird's simple
song lifts a burst of joy into the rising day,

rhyming the light and tuning the silences.
And still the heart sings.

THE LONGER LURE

Do not worry about tomorrow,
for tomorrow will bring worries of its own.
—Jesus of Nazareth

These sparrows keep their vigil
without regard for our noticing,

their song a riff of short bursts
against the heavier weight of

city noise—a force of instinct,
a witness to interior delight,

a passion of their little heart,
who can say? They wait for

us and watch, hoping that
some scrap might fall from a

generous or negligent hand,
living by habits of hunger as

we also know to do, and by
the longer lure of hope.

When Words Are Not Enough

Silence, healing.
      —Heraclitus

There are days like this when words
are not enough: not strong enough to

hold the late-autumn light as it glazes
the last leaves that cling to the maple

by the house; not tender enough to stir
long untouched skin with a trace—and

more—of breath; not bold enough to
heal a hurt long past and gone; not free

enough to wake us to the wildness we
were made to taste. There are days

like this, and nights, when words give
way to a silence truer than all we know,

a wisdom holding us until we become
the song we thought was ours to find.

Something Left Behind

This morning a wedge of geese drifts
out across the silky-mannered sky,

all blue and vast and beckoning,
the drift of their October flight

a sign of the coming cold, and as
I watch them steering in this wide

arc they hesitate for a moment and
then turn slowly north again, as if

remembering something left behind
across the distances. Listening, I

wander with them, in my mind, to
places where I'd also once found

and lost some traces of the harvest
of love, and sorrow clouds my

memory as I hear the last echoes
of a song receding and now gone,

while the geese fly on, drawn by
what lures them finally home.

Different Ways to Dream

*—remembering a painting by Carl Spitzweg in the Neue
Pinakothek, Munich*

Are you a poet? a neighbor asks with blunt force.
I stumble along in awkward silence, not knowing

what to say, then smile as I suddenly remember
the painting of "The Poor Poet" I'd once seen:

there, lying beneath blankets heaped in piles
on his disheveled bed, this word-crazed dreamer

seems hard at work, a feathered pen clenched
between his teeth while with upturned fingers

he seems poised in the hunt for a fugitive word,
his mind searching for a fitting image or phrase,

caught up in the weave of sound and sense he
hopes to coax into rhythmed lines and rhymes.

He's fixed an umbrella above his head against
the rains that pierce the roof, while at his side

a pile of old books is close enough to grasp;
sunlight spills through an unopened window

into the room where he sits, and a well-worn
boot stands near the cold *Kachelofen* like

a soldier at attention, with crumpled sheets
of paper stuffed into the oven's gaping mouth—

discarded drafts of poems, perhaps, waiting
like love to be changed into flame and song.

Meanwhile, one of my cats saunters quietly
into the room where I sit and muse and sprawls

herself out in my lap, reminding me of other
languages of love and different ways to dream.

What Widening

At winter's deep the bitter cold
slows the morning race of time,

the shining cloudless skies giving
chase to the night's reluctant dark,

and as usual the day makes no
complaint of its own but goes on

attending to its untethered ways,
while the hours drift slowly on

and by, and yet they leave a crease
of stillness—for madness or for

mercy, who can say? All this comes
when and how it will, because it must,

and when it does it opens us to what
we need to brave the stinging cold.

And what of us? What profit or gain
will all our restless worry bring us?

What widening of heart will sing us?

Part of the Whole

Sing the gardens, my heart, that you don't know,
like those poured into glass, radiant, unattainable.
Fountains of Isfahan and roses of Shiraz: bless them
singing, and praise them, each and all, incomparable.

Show, my heart, that you can't live without them,
that their figs are ripening just for you,
that you mingle with them as the breezes
stir their blossoming branches, caress your face.

Avoid the thought that anything's lacking
in what you've decided—to be!
As silken thread you're woven into this weave.

Whatever image you've joined yourself to in your heart,
even if only in a moment of life's anguish, see how
it's part of the whole, this glorious tapestry.

—RAINER MARIA RILKE

TRANSLATED BY MARK S. BURROWS

An Everlasting Yes

After the final no there comes a yes,
And on that yes the future world depends.

—WALLACE STEVENS

THE PROMISE OF GREEN

Another spring stirs from winter's hold,
with the hoped-for and hidden waiting

to be revealed. Once more songbirds
return to fill the crease of morning with

the radiance of their song, their music
drifting about among trees thick with

silence and the promise of green, and
I want to believe that love is stronger

than death and forgiveness deeper
than the habits of hate, and I want to

know that what now lasts and always
will is the lure of an everlasting yes.

EPIPHANIES

—at L'Aroma Café, on Newbury Street (Boston)

Most days I wonder when and how they'll come,
the epiphanies, but on this August morning I find

myself sitting at an outdoor café with a book that
ponders *Why Poetry Matters*, how it helps make

visible the truths we sense but cannot see, which
sing us beyond the long *et cetera* of small virtues,

and then I notice them: a family of sparrows all
brown and bustle and hop, glancing about nervously

with their soft swiveling heads, intent on their work
with what seems like gleeful bursts of gladness.

With studied devotion they stalk the flowerboxes
one by one, filled to overflowing with petunias—

pink and purple and white—plucking their silky
heads one petal at a time, tasting a beauty we

but dimly see, and only with our eyes.

This Radiance

It is late afternoon and already the sun is
beginning to sink low over the western hills,

warming the ground still damp from weeks
of rain, as the drifting slant of light dazzles

the silken threads strung among the spikes of
grass by the spring's first spiders to emerge,

and hosts of gnats dart about with crazy joy
in the late-day light, not knowing anything

about yesterday or having a thought about
tomorrow. They live on as they do in each

moment given them in their short-lived
lives, sensing in their way as I do in mine

a measure of the happiness I find as I lie
in this moist grass without a single worry,

and begin to sense the yes that dwells
in all this, that holds each single part in

the embrace of some larger whole—along
with the plenitude of grasses and spiders,

of sun and gnats, and all that lives on
in the abundance of this radiance.

Amid Durations

Every beloved thing becomes the being of its praise.
By loving the things of this world, one learns to praise
the world: one enters into the cosmos of the word.
—Gaston Bachelard

The clouds know more of light
with its restless flow and racing

speed than we do who try to
calculate what lies within

the velocity of our surprise;
they make their way out across

the spreading skies, throwing
shadows on all that wanders

below their shifting shapes
of black and gray. Their days

consist of drifting play, and
what they know of constancy

is change. Unlike us they do
not pause to wonder about

any of this, but seem to praise
in their own wordless way

the flow of time amid durations
that are only ours to surmise.

STILL

But when I love you, what do I love? It is not physical beauty nor
temporal glory nor the brightness of light dear to earthly eyes,
nor the sweet melodies of all kinds of songs, nor the gentle odor
of flowers and ointments and perfumes, nor manna or honey,
nor limbs welcoming the embraces of the flesh. It is not these I
love when I love my God. Yet. . .
—Augustine of Hippo

They're still among us, the miracles,
even when we no longer notice them
in the clutter and clutch of our minds.

You once asked me how we come to
know them, and when, and why? I'm
never quite sure, but surely not just

on sun-drenched April mornings when
the meadow gleams with daffodils and
the wind is ripe with lilac and hyacinth.

Then, of course, but also in seasons
when we thirst for what we no longer
have and long to taste and see again.

And still they're close at hand, shining
in this crazy lumpen world, and still
they lure us with song despite what we

face of suffering, unshadowing the day
and parading through the night, an inward
kind of radiance that still might save us.

THE INSIDE CURVE OF SPEECH

*. . .Yet there is a light I love, and a food, and a kind of
embrace when I love my God.*
—*Augustine of Hippo*

Each time I catch a glimpse of glory shining,
as it sometimes does, in ordinary things—

on the bright surfaces of leaves and in what
binds us in the dark weight of the night, in

the faces of the neglected and despised and
and all the other creatures and things that

fill the void of this earth with song and reach
up to the heights of the highest heavens—

I know that nothing can be as it once was,
merely complicated or important, and that I,

too, am made for an unworded kind of praise
carved into the inside curve of speech, and I

come to see how all the things of this life
long for a stillness beyond the restless grind

of thought, and I sense that I, too, will one day
be loosed of my body with its bundle of care

and dare to reach for what the heron knows
and the deer, and the snail who bears aloft

her little tight-coiled house. Each shares
a measure of a greater radiance, each opens

to a light that shines within, each chances
what it takes to seek the long way home.

CONVERGENCE

All desire is for a part of oneself gone missing,
or so it feels to the person in love.
—*Anne Carson*

It wasn't just the fire consuming us
like two flaming trees leaning into

each other, their unfurling leaves
and curling bark yielding to heat

and the luminous burn of desire.
This, but also the unspoken joys

that breathe in a wild descent of
tongues, a convergence of speech

as on the first Pentecost, and more,
a witness to a truth we somehow

know beyond what we can ever
finally say: that love descends on

us in our longings, gathering us
in ties stronger than what binds

us still within, a gift we'll one day
taste as a beginning at every end.

CREATIO EX SILENTIO

Silence into word into wind into rain
into river into wave into earth into grain
into mercy into grief into blood into vein
into flesh into love into tears into gain.

Where Love Waits

The best things can't be shown.
—Gioia Timpanelli

Be always ready to fail at
something large or small,

to leave undone some
unessential task and claim

the possibilities of your mind
to give yourself to the wildness

of your heart where love
desires you just as you are.

Be impatient with the silent
surfaces of things and dare

the depths, courting sorrow
and joy with an equal hope.

For this is the song that
leads you finally home

where you'll find yourself
when you've missed your way,

and this is where love waits
for all who're never finally

lost but ever found over and
over again in the seeking.

Beneath the Surfaces

See how the heights now fall into the waiting eye,
this fling of unspun wind and blue-dazzled sky

that shimmers with the dance of summer-swept
leaves as they go drifting ablaze and idly by.

And look, hope is not some calculable force
against the steady gains of night, and love

is more than what we can measure or finally
know; these join us beyond what we deserve

and lead us into paths of agony and delight,
and, no, never pause to ask how or ever why.

And know this, too: that life flows on beneath
the surfaces of what we dimly have and lose,

searching here and there for some wedge of
rest for the weary heart, carrying traces of

a song that sings with a never-failing yes.

A Second Life

The day doesn't always rise into laughter
or light, often stumbling into shadows

so dark we can't see anything, not even
the outline of our outstretched hands held

right before our face. In such times there
is little that consoles us and nothing of

the clarities that lighten our way on gentler
days, as if caught up in storms that strain

the dikes of order and propriety we'd
so carefully built to keep hold of our

wild and restless souls. And yet the dark
draws us to long for light, reminds us that

we have room for a second life, timeless
and wide, beyond what might have been

or still could be, where nothing, not even
death, can stay the tides of love again.

Nothing Less

*—a late-afternoon reverie in Taizé, on a gentle hill
  looking westward*

The world of things is what it is, no more or less,
yet we imagine we're more important than the rest—

like trees rooted where a seed once fell, aspiring to no
other place or nobler form, or winds that blow wherever

they will without a trace of fear; like well-worn stones
that lie here and there in the field where I idly sit, warmed

all day by the late-spring sun, or the flow of the creek that
I can see but not hear, swollen by weeks of steady rain.

Across the gleaming field a herd of cows stands grazing
contentedly, giving themselves to the day's needs without

a single thought, while on and on a swoop of swallows darts
through clouds of gnats that come from no place I could see.

All these are what they are without a worry in the world—
as we also long to be who are often uneasy with our lives;

each lives within a presence not theirs alone, each seeking
nothing less than the ordinary miracle of everything.

THE DARK WAY HOME

Words are not much to speak about when all
is said and done, bits of sound shaped by teeth

and tongue and carried by breath and habit, in
stray feelings and the many postures of the mind.

Their treasures often hide in plain sight among
ordinary things, their roots deep enough to endure

the long durations of drought; they bear the risks
of love, with all its gifts, luring us to wander out

past the dark cottages of common sense. So dare
to reach for them as you do for lights that mark

the long way home; let them open you to what
the heart desires among what lasts, and welcome

them like rains that sometimes fall in desert heat
to meet the earth's thirst and yours—like long-lost

dreams or new-found joys bold enough to shake
you from your shadowed fears. Listen for them

in the stillnesses until they become like old sequoia
seeds that have lain for centuries, waiting for fire

to break them open to release a tender rise of
greening shoots which reach out to fill the skies

with the magnificence of a great towering tree.

STILL LIFE

is what it is, as here
in this Italian bowl:

one apple with a
single wrinkled leaf

clinging to the stem,
a twist of gnarly ginger

and two shining
ripe lemons.

Still life is just what
it is, despite our

strongest longings
or deepest fears:

it is not indifferent
to us through

all the years, and
doesn't wait for some

gesture of assent to rise
from the mind's deep,

but simply keeps
what is still life,

as rain to earth,
wind to cloud,

as grass to field,
hope to heart.

VITA CONTEMPLATIVA

Even a soul submerged in sleep is hard at work,
and helps make something of the world.
—Heraclitus

On a day when I should be working
on other things, I find myself sitting

quietly in a sun-soaked chair in
the living room, my hands cradling

a hot cup of tea, the lace curtains
swaying in the morning breeze,

my thoughts drifting like a softly
rippling stream drawn onward by

the physics of flow. And all along
my cats have wedged themselves

beside me in this overstuffed chair,
for comfort or for warmth—and

who can blame them? They seem
to dream as we do, curled around

each other, as we also long to be,
not thinking to wonder why it is

I've ceased my work to join them
in their reverie, or if I'm happy

with my life, or any other
useless thought at all.

Beyond this Haste

Late have I loved you, beauty at once so ancient and so new . . .
—*Augustine of Hippo*

No moment in this life lasts, yet none is ever lost,
each wrinkle in time held in an ever-onward flow,

like a rain-soaked stream that tumbles down, rippling
over stone and fallen branch with a will that does

not slow or cease, or the restlessness we often feel;
each particle of time is this and more, wandering on

in its steady forward pull, yet all of it seeking rest as
we also do who long for a measure of peace beyond

this haste, a glimpse of radiance never far but one
we often only dimly face or learn to love too late.

AWAITING

Margins are what we need, what silence
offers us among the words we use, like

a target awaiting the arrow's strike or
a bare canvas longing for color and form

and line, like a blank page that waits for
the first words of a poem we don't yet

even know to write or spaces where we
find ourselves bound to a whole we see

faintly, if at all, and then only in part.

Visitation

To think a flower is to see and smell it,
And to eat a fruit is to know its meaning.
—*Fernando Pessoa*

You come bearing gifts
and prophecy: eyes moist

with wondering, courage
to share what is not ours

to keep, and a red mango
ripened on a far shore,

the fragrance of here and
now and coming sweet.

Beneath this Glory

A delight to my eyes are glowing and pleasant colors. They
touch me, wide awake, throughout the day, nor do they
give me a moment's respite in the way the voices of
singers, sometimes the entire choir, keep silence.
  —*Augustine of Hippo*

Again the colors begin their blaze, veiled
all summer under a dense canopy of green,

their bold reds and oranges and golds
flaming the blue harvest sky. Beneath this

glory I seek my way home at last, the winds
beginning to unburden the trees of their

thousand shimmering wicks that burn one
last time before winter finally will come,

ushering in a cold that stings flesh grown
lazy under the charm of this September sun.

Soon enough these trees will stand as bony
skeletons once more, their afternoon shadows

reaching out with long entangled fingers
across the yard, their autumn dress falling

to be raked into mounds and burned, only to
rise again in a plume of sweet smoke and ash.

Wandering out beneath their uplifted arms,
I sense something of a movement that carries

all of this with us unceasingly, each shining
moment caught in this endless drift of time,

now briefly here but soon to be finished and
gone, awaiting the rise of another coming year.

Waiting Emptiness

In the realm of imagination, every immanence
takes on transcendence.
—Gaston Bachelard

December arrives with the unbent force
of gravity, driving steady sheets of rain

that sting the face and soak us to the bone;
amidst all this the trees keep a silent watch,

not uttering a single word, their branches
bare now, brushing each other across

respectful distances, stripped of what
they'd worn in greener months gone by.

The piercing dark of these early winter
nights reminds us to seek the company

of comforting things—a crackling fire
in the woodstove, the light dancing on

walls and ceiling, our cats curled up just
close enough to be satisfied, and well

loved sweaters taken out of storage again,
the mothballed scent tickling our nose.

All these ready us to join this season,
to loose our disguise and step out naked

and new into winter's waiting emptiness.

NINE FORMS OF LIGHT

There is no Paradise, no place of true completion,
that does not include within its walls the unknown.
—Jane Hirshfield

1

A burst of the stove's blue flame,
shadows leaping suddenly
into the dark of an unlit kitchen,
a single old chair by the table,
a clean-swept floor,
an unsaid word;

2

the strike of a match, two men
turning away from cold night winds,
a hollow large as hunger
staining their faces, their hands
cupped hard against the cold
that settles its ache into the heart;

3

the first crease of the morning,
the veil lifted from what
the ordered eye knows,
a solitary blackbird
flinging song recklessly
into the dim but brightening sky;

4

midday, and across the square a gull
holds court alone on a high balustrade,
ignores the sea's surging groan,
the recklessness of wind and wave,
the sun flaming her shining wings
and the whole swirling dance below;

5

and why, if the matter of light belongs
to the science of particles and waves,
do we suppose that it is other than
a source of gladness within us which
sometimes grasps what the eye
can never finally reach;

6

not the weight of sorrow
which pulls with its own gravity,
but the brightening
that begins to form
in each moment caught
between hesitance and hope;

7

in its full spectrum it is cadmium,
turquoise, and every other hue,
names for what turns the dark aside,
what greets eyes startled by winter's
descending dusk as again the skies
bow to the rise of cobalt majesty;

8

another season of sorrows,
a single candle announcing its
arrival, joining the others to keep
a lonely vigil before the darkened
icon of the Virgin who does not smile,
having seen all this before;

9

a winter's night on a country lane,
one farmhouse after another bathed
in the half-moon's brittle glow, the blue
flicker of late-night television glazing
the glass from within, meeting starlight
that has raced across magnitudes of space.

SLOW ART

> *Things keep their secrets.*
> —*Heraclitus*

Week by week she comes to the foot of the old maple
by our house, this girl of eight assembling odds and

ends of things—twigs, beads, bits of moss, shards
of glass—to build a fairy house. One day she tears

it all apart, this intricate dwelling place she'd made
with an architect's studied care, leaving behind a

pile of rubble she now scorns as childish fantasy.
And then, on a gentler day, she returns to the debris

to piece it back together again, a new form rising
from the ruins, not with a builder's skills but as

a slow art, a kind of wordless sacrifice of praise.

STILL THE WINDS

Once I thought questions held the answers I needed,
though the winds know no notion of such an opinion,

or the cows who graze so peacefully here in this field
where I idly sit, like those I often walked beside in

the lazy summers of my youth. Then, the answers
seemed secure; some satisfied and others not—and

still the winds blew through the restless waiting trees,
and still the cows stood their ground. The questions

remained, knowing nothing of the fickle mind with
its wandering ways, and the years came and went,

taking the answers with them. And now, as I sense
the life behind me across far more decades than I

will know again, the questions drift like the winds
in their indeterminate way—now here and then

gone, rustling the leaves as they go, whether or not
I pause to listen, while the cows chew on, satisfied.

What Keeps Us

—for Adelphia Martinez, Maria "Tsee Pin"; San Ildefonso
Pueblo, New Mexico

The town seems deserted, the stillness interrupted by
a few dogs who wander toward us with halting gait,
untroubled by fear; in the middle of the empty square,
a single towering cottonwood keeps its long watch, its
roots reaching deep into the earth, its branches spread
wide as if to supplicate the gods or gather the rain that
sometimes falls with the tears of those who live here.
On this April morning the air is still cool, but already
the sun is throwing hot shadows down upon the dust,
and I imagine what summer will bring of heat and
loneliness to this place.
                          It was her withered hands that
first drew my eyes, this old woman who'd been shaping
the "black on black" pots since childhood, molding
and then carving these clay vessels before setting them
in a shallow firepit to bake for days as the embers cool,
the heat hardening them slowly until they're ready to
be painted—with eagles and snakes and things that
live in the legends the elders tell. I watch as she takes
a lump of moist red clay, working it slowly in her
hands, and tells me how her pots keep the stories
alive, these tales told through the generations by those
who know to reverence the spirit of sun and rain, of
earth and wind, creatures and stones, memories
worn smooth as river rocks tumbled through endless

seasons of suffering—*the young don't know much about this anymore*, she says.

She leans over a small pot, picking it up carefully with her wise hands. *That one's special— it tells the first story my father ever taught me,* and turns to search in a drawer until she finds a yellowed photograph of him, standing by a carving he'd made of himself as a warrior, his body painted and clothed with leather and brightly beaded feathers; she holds the card a long time, gazing into his face, then sets it down on the table, placing the small black pot in my hands: *We think it's ours to remember them,* she says looking away, *but they're what keeps us.*

I cradle it in my hands, tracing my fingers along the carvings etched into its side, and ask about her art. *It's my life,* she says quietly, her eyes gazing out across the empty square, and, after a long silence, *I do it because it brings peace.* Across the room an old dog leans hard against the weathered wooden door, and somewhere far off a child cries.

Beyond the Maps

—for Sean and the tenders of Poet's Corner in Adelaide

Again we find ourselves gathered by poems,
by language shaped in the wide and spacious

silences beyond our naming, a handful of words
thrown onto the canvas of the old certainties—

ambitions of war and other efficiencies of state,
and the politics of greed that drive the brokers

of this world. And we, sheltering under tents
of metaphor and desire, refuse the seduction

of their strategies, setting out on paths whose
ends we cannot see, steering our way home

beyond the maps they've given us, gathering
crumbs that will be enough to make a feast.

A Gaze Not Ours

When I look at your heavens, the work of your fingers,
the moon and the stars that you have established,
what are human beings. . .? (Ps. 8:4)

Once, near midnight on a clear and moonless night,
I paddled out of the harbor into the vast stretch of sea,

my little canoe tossed about by the pulling tides, pushed
here and there by the ceaseless groan of wind and wave,

and suddenly felt the immensity of it all—above, the night
sky strewn with a hundred million stars, and beneath,

the mirroring darkness of the surging depths. And as I
rode the rising swells I sensed how fragile this life is,

how each part belongs somehow to a larger living whole,
and how we're caught between infinities we but dimly

sense and never fully know. Who are we amid such
immensities of space as these, and what does our soul

hold of the light that races shimmering through the skies?
What do we ever have but glimpses, now and then, of

a gaze not ours, between inscrutable origins and ends?
And what do we know of how we belong to any of this,

how even what we fear and long for are somehow part
of these ebbing surfaces and this ever flowing deep?

THAT GENTLE KINGDOM

Today I spent idly considering the lilies
blooming promiscuously along the road,

watching them so closely I could almost
see how they must have stepped forth

from the winter earth's crusty shell;
despite their flashy show of radiance

they make no demand of us, arriving
without ambition or any hope of gain.

Tell me, what else should I have done?
They take no notice of us in their gentle

swaying ways, stirred by the winds,
perhaps by love—who can say? In all

this they're unlike us in our search for
status or chance permanence of place,

and in the spell of their dance they spice
the winds with a fragrance that draws

butterflies and bees alike, belonging to
that gentle kingdom where the last will

be first and the meek inherit the earth.
And what of you? Do you know how to

take your place in the family of things?
Will you dare to turn and step aside

from the march toward importance,
to care enough to save your life, at least

a little, and brush the hems of glory as
they come close and pass you by?

This Somewhere

There must be a place where no one wonders
whether you belong, where even your cares

are joined by wind and cloud in their reverie,
and this somewhere could be here and now,

and is for some, though far removed from all
who must face their pain without relief and

wait for light to break the spell of their long
nights and shadowed days. And all at once

I notice a pioneer weed rising at the edge of
the city lot I walk by each day, a corner strewn

with shards of glass and choked with neglect
as deep as a stubborn late-November fog.

And there, atop a greening blade, a single
yellow flower comes to crown this unlikely

majesty, a reminder that not even the grit
of loss or the grind of grief can ever

finally stay the chance of home.

ONLY THE SONG

Though the world changes shape
as swiftly as the drifting clouds,
all that's whole comes home
to the most ancient things.

Beyond what changes and passes
on, farther and freer than this,
your primal song endures,
God playing upon the lyre.

We've not grasped what suffering means,
nor have we learned to love,
and what takes us in death
is not unveiled.
Only the song, drifting across the land,
consecrates and celebrates.

—RAINER MARIA RILKE

TRANSLATED BY MARK S. BURROWS

Afterword
A BRIEF BIOGRAPHY OF THIS BOOK

How this collection came to be is a long story. The writing began some years ago when I was living in New England, progressed through a move to the American Southwest, and came to completion in Germany. Strangely, the trajectory of this journey brings the pattern of my grandparents' story full circle: they emigrated in the early 1920s, then only in their late teens, from a clock-making town on the edge of the Black Forest to a city on the outskirts of Chicago. But the poems gathered here are not about this, at least not explicitly, even while they carry allusions to this changing horizon—from New England to New Mexico and finally on to Old Europe. Their primary interest explores the inner movements and outer rhythms that reach across geographical boundaries, even while being firmly rooted in place. Above all, they point to what it is that abides amidst the changes: the resilience of children's laughter and the resonance of sorrow's tears; the endurance of birdsong and the constancy of seasonal rhythms; acts of unexpected generosity joining us in our differences and the creativity that belongs to our essential nature.

Here, the words of Rainer Maria Rilke from one of the poems included in this volume ring true:

> But this march of time—
> it's of little worth among
> what ever abides.

What is of great worth, in the midst of life's impermanence and our restlessness, has to do with the deeper continuities—"what *ever* abides"—that carry us through what changes. They are the treasure that deepens us when we leave the familiar behind and dare to open ourselves to what we do not yet know. The poems bear witness to this abiding, listening patiently for traces of the rhyme that holds the song, even in the silences. They arise from and address an inner longing, one that endures in the face of what comes—and goes—in our lives.

The title of this volume gestures toward this, suggesting how our experience of the "abiding" is marked both by our longing for stability and by our awareness of our fragility. But how it came to be was startling, mirroring the mysterious manner in which poems themselves often rise into language from the unconscious. In fact, it came to me well into the writing process, and long after the last of the poems was finished; until then, it was nowhere in my mind. During the early going, several others presented themselves, and among these *Epiphanies* seemed most fitting—as it happens, the title of one of the poems and a theme descriptive of the collection as a whole. But this was not to be: at this late stage, a phrase taken from the closing line of one of the last poems to be written—"the chance of home"— suddenly struck me, intuitively, as being exactly right. And that was that.

That the title came at this juncture cannot gainsay the fact that it captured something essential to the volume as I had begun to understand it. On the formal level, the poems bear witness to outer transitions, from the "new world" back to the "old." But even in this they remind us that place is only one of the markers for home, since its sense emerges not only at the end of a move but all along the way. Immigrants know this, my grandparents among them, in their search for home in an unfamiliar land and uncertain times. But so do migratory birds together with species compelled to wander because of the crisis brought on by climate change. We often discover what "home" means only when we've left the familiar behind, often against our will, in our search for refuge. These poems bear witness to this adaptability, on the one hand, and to the determination to hold onto what abides against the forces of disruption and change, on the other.

Of course, the essential simplicity of what "home" means also points to its inherent complexity, since it is ultimately an *experience* and not simply a *place*. One might think of it as functioning like the *basso continuo* of the Baroque, the bass voice in contrapuntal music which we sense even though it is rarely exposed. As the deep "ground," it stabilizes the movement of the whole by undergirding it. It is a kind of ballast, to mix metaphors, that holds the little ship of our life aright amid the shifting currents of wind and wave. Its purpose has more in common with the hidden keel and the unseen rudder than with the billowing show of sails. Its power does not propel us, but helps us keep our direction when adrift on the open seas of life.

What emerged of this sense as these poems took shape was not, then, something I was thinking about as I wrote. It is, though, the conviction that holds the parts together under the sway of a larger whole, rooted not on the surfaces but in the heart of things. It comes to us, when it does, from the depth of the unconscious, the moorings where poetry discovers the resilience of its proper voice. We often come to understand what this sense means, and how it shapes us, when we have left or lost the familiar—whether freely or by force of circumstance, by choice or by chance. It holds us in the midst of dis*place*ment, inviting us to see that home has to do with discovering *how* and not *where* we belong.

At our best, we come to recognize how important it is to cultivate this chance, not for our sake alone but on behalf of an inclusive whole. How we commit ourselves to this vision is not something we can know about in theory, or in advance; it emerges from day to day in the basic gestures of responsibility we take for others and in our need, with them, of common care. It comes in myriad ways, among them the simple acts of hospitality—given or received—that illumine this life like bursts of light arising out of the dark. It carries assurances capable of sustaining us through hard times and in difficult places. It leans on the courage that inspires us to risk going forward in the face of diminishment, loss, and even death. The sense of home reveals itself often enough in a kind of intuitive knowing whose center lies beyond the margins of the familiar, often at the edges of language itself. In such diverse ways we come to recognize it as a matter of chance and not as a fixed certainty. Those forced to migrate because of war or some other tragedy know this.

This chance is thus a wager on resilience, taking shape as the source of an inner endurance, a courage rooted in our vulnerability. We, along with the other creatures of this earth, seem to be somehow "hard-wired" for it. How does it come to us? The poems in the three sections of this collection suggest that it does so by inviting us to undertake "a long listening," often for what we do not deserve to hope for or know to expect; to seek what rings "as true as song" in the midst of the confusions and contradictions we face; and, to open ourselves to "an everlasting yes" that is the gospel of life. Implicitly, these echo the ancient trivium of faith, hope, and love, a pattern deeply engrained in the Christian tradition, but our experience of this dynamic is not limited to creed or bound by confession. And the fact that we come to know the power of these truths in the midst of change, often *in extremis*, should not surprise us. For as Wallace Stevens reminds us in memorable lines from "Sunday Morning,"

> Death is the mother of beauty; hence from her,
> Alone, shall come fulfillment to our dreams
> And our desires.

The chance of home is a vital part of what beckons us when we have lost our way. Our experience of it reminds us that our failures, and death itself, can become an unexpected gift, turning us from the "habitual preoccupations where we seek only what we already know, in advance, what we can find without changing, without having to change," as Jean-Louis Chrétien put it. Such preoccupations, as we know, are as exhausting as they are futile; in contrast, what this chance offers is the vision and strength to do the most significant thing: to change *ourselves*. Hence, the wager of this chance is not only about home. It is about *us* and what we know to make of it.

These poems point to this gift, often tangible only when we understand it as a *chance*—for us and for others with us. They suggest, at least implicitly, that this arises from an experience we can neither determine nor explain, coming to us from the deep wellspring of mystery. They remind us that the choice of this gift holds us in a larger whole, together with others and the myriad species which inhabit this world. They welcome us into this surprise—and, yes, into the epiphanies—not through a dependence on some special experience but rather by calling us to indwell what *is*. The Portuguese poet Fernando Pessoa captures this well in the form of an invitation:

Let's pay attention only to where we are,
There's enough beauty in being here and not somewhere else.

These are wise words. They remind us that the depth of our lives—the source of our true home—depends less on external circumstances than on our attentiveness to them. The generosity of this chance, and this alone, beckons us to experience beauty in this life, and the beauty of this life, even when this seems not at all evident, or altogether unlikely. Perhaps especially then.

Is this a wistful call for a "reenchantment" of the world? Perhaps, and surely so when our longing for what we lack awakens our neglected sense of wonder. When we learn to stand again, as children do, in amazement at what is—and that there is anything at all, to recall Wittgenstein's description of the mystical. When we come to know that home is where the heart is, as an old adage puts it. Such openness, such a second naiveté, keeps us open to this chance. It reminds us to stake our fate on a sense of home spacious enough, in the places of our wandering, to make room for others in theirs.

The poems gathered here thus gesture toward this "common sense" of home. In so doing they remind us of something significant and even urgent, not merely for our flourishing but for our very survival in such times as these when this seems an increasingly imperiled vision, weakened by growing indifference, at one extreme, and threatened by the violence of exclusivist commitments—to nation, class, or religion—at the other. For only as we inhabit this world as a common*place*, only as we learn to cherish it as a way of mutual belonging, does this chance seem hopeful—for ourselves, in the midst of our diversities, and with others and other species of our world. How this happens is a story one could tell in countless ways, most rooted in the kind of undramatic moments these poems recall: in the chance encounter with a street percussionist plying his trade in a Lisbon subway; amid a flourish of birdsong overheard as the night releases its mantle of silence; in the image of a long unused temple bell that "still sings in the silences."

What undergirds these poems is the realization that our very lives, together with all that inhabits this world, depend upon the chance of home. They remember that whatever song we make as humans is never isolated or alone, but joins the primordial melodies of wind and storm, of lion's roar and birdsong. And if the witness to such convergences falls under Ruskin's indictment as a "pathetic fallacy," then so be it. It could also just be the voicing of a truth nearly forgotten, but deeply essential, regarding the common home we share—with all those "others" we find ourselves among on this planet. It is a chance as precious as it is precarious, a hope we share with all that lives and breathes, flies and crawls and swims. Of all that simply *is*. Call it the rule of interdependence, the desire to honor our essential connectedness. Call it a sense of belonging across our differences, for the sake of the whole. Call it our primal longing for comfort. Call it the chance of home.

Mark S. Burrows

ACKNOWLEDGMENTS

Grateful acknowledgement is made to the following publications in which earlier versions of these poems first appeared:

AMOS: "Three Silences," published as "Dreimal Stille" in a German translation by Carlota Raul with Ian Pollock; an earlier version of it first appeared as the featured "poem of the day," in October, 2004, on the "Poets against the War" website, curated by Sam Hamill

Anglican Theological Review: "Convergence"

Arts: "So, Too, the Heart" and "Beneath Our Speech"

The Cortland Review: "In Answer" and "Still Life"

Eremos (Australia): "Magpie Praise"

91st Meridian: "What Lingers" from Rainer Maria Rilke's *Sonnets to Orpheus* I.22 (untitled in the original)

The Paraclete Poetry Anthology. Selected and New Poems, 2005-2016: "Entrance" ("Eingang"), from *The Book of Images* by Rainer Maria Rilke (author's translation)

Presence. A Journal of Catholic Poetry, "First Listening" and "A Few of the Particulars"

Seasons of a New Heart. Poets' Corner Anthology (Adelaide, South Australia): "Beyond the Maps" and "Magpie Praise"

Seminary Ridge Review: "Something Left Behind" (originally entitled "The Coming Dark")

Southern Quarterly: "Despite the Odds"

Spiritus: "Still the Heart"

The lines from Heraclitus included as epigrams in a number of the poems are from *Fragments. The Collected Wisdom of Heraclitus*, translated by Brooks Haxton with a Foreword by James Hillman (New York: Viking, 2001); those from Fernando Pessoa are from a volume edited and translated by Richard Zenith, *A Little Larger than the Entire Universe. Selected Poems* (New York and London: Penguin, 2006). The translations of Rilke's poems—"Entrance" ("Eingang," in *The Book of Images*) and three of *The Sonnets to Orpheus* ("What Lingers" [I.22], "Part of the Whole" [II.21], and "Only the Song" [I.19], all untitled in the original)—are mine.

*

I am grateful to Paraclete Press for accepting this volume for publication, now some five years ago. Since that time, several moves and the call to a professorship in Bochum postponed my completion of the manuscript. I am grateful to Jon M. Sweeney, Publisher, together with Robert Edmonson, Managing Editor, and Michelle Rich and Sr. Antonia Cleverly in production and marketing, respectively, for their patience and good counsel along the way.

Many friends and colleagues have offered advice and encouragement during the years I have devoted to writing this collection. Among them, I am grateful to my spouse, Ute Molitor, who read and commented on early drafts, and, more significantly, journeyed with me from our longtime home in Boston first to Albuquerque and then on to Bochum, a "long and winding road" that marked a glad return to Germany for us both. All along the way she shared with me what the chance of home means, as both wager and gift; to her, first of all, my deep and abiding thanks.

Many others read or heard versions of these poems along the way, often in workshops and retreats I've led over the years. I am grateful to my Australian friend Sean Gilbert, who invited me "down under" to speak on poetry and spirituality and lead various events under the auspices of the Effective Living Center and Christ Church in Adelaide. These events gave birth to a monthly gathering, "Poet's Corner," a meeting of poets and lovers of poetry to share new work and talk about the craft of writing. Several other Australians from Sydney have also enriched my life in profound ways, both as friends and as fellow artists: Doug Purnell, a painter and professor of pastoral theology; Stephanie Dowrick, conversation partner in all things poetic—above all, Rilke—who directs the Universal Heart Network; and, Trish Watts, cofounder of InterPlay Australia, who knows to heed Rilke's admonition to "dance the orange"—and so much else. My thanks, too, to members of the "Rilke circle" who met regularly in our Cambridge home while I was translating the poems that became *Prayers of a Young Poet* (Paraclete Press, 2016), for their good counsel and encouragement.

I am also glad to mention friends on both sides of the Atlantic whose presence has held me in recent years: first of all, Gotthard Fermor, my theopoetical companion who invited me to join the "Bonn Rilke Projekt" shortly after I returned to Germany, and has shared so much of this journey in friendship since; those whose love and support sustained me through the hard times, above all my parents, family, and friends—among whom Rick Chrisman, Robert Jonas, Connie Lasher, John and Liz Ohlson, Jennifer Rossetti, Carl

Scovel, Willie Sordillo, and Josie von Zitzewitz bear special mention; and, finally, my students at the university, especially those who participated in the American poetry seminars I've taught in recent years, among whom Marie Heyder, who signed on for the first of these seminars, and Carlota Raul, my student assistant for several years, bear special mention and thanks.

I am glad to acknowledge three institutions whose tangible support facilitated my work on this volume. My thanks, first, to the Santa Fe Art Institute for inviting me for a writing residency in 2013, together with the Witter Bynner Poetry Foundation for a fellowship that sponsored that residency. Second, my thanks to the St. Botolph Club of Boston where I had the good fortune to be elected an Arts Associate Member from 2008–2011; alongside the remarkable program of cultural offerings for its members, the highlight of my association with this distinguished institution—a club that counts Robert Frost, together with many other celebrated writers and artists, among its past members—was meeting Kwesi Budu-Arthur, Paulina Drummond, Peter Lyons, and Mark Wolf, who became treasured friends and wonderful companions over the years. Third, my thanks to the Protestant University of Applied Sciences in Bochum (Evangelische Hochschule Rheinland-Westfalen-Lippe), for granting a sabbatical leave in 2017–18, which enabled me to complete work on this volume. I am grateful to my colleagues here, and particularly Desmond Bell, Wolfgang Maaser, Gerhard Schäfer, Tobi Klug, Arian Schiffer-Nasserie, Didi Sachser, Marlies Hendricks, Rainer Lienemann, and Helene Skladny, for their generous welcome and gracious embrace of my work as scholar, teacher, and poet.

Finally, I am profoundly grateful for my colleague and friend Robin Jensen, who conspired with me and others in establishing the Summer Institute for Theology and the Arts and guiding its life for almost two decades in Boston. This was a remarkable institution in its day, a creative two-week residential event that brought poets and painters, dancers and sculptors, musicians and puppeteers, together with theologians and philosophers, students and pastors, to create a passionate community of the arts. That collaboration over the years, together with the companionship of Lisa Di Franza and Ellen Oak, did much to shape my life and encourage my work as a poet. More recently, I am grateful for my friends among the "Bochumer Literaten" (www.bochumerliteraten.de), and above all fellow poet Anton Schlösser of that circle, friend and partner in wide-ranging conversations about poetry and culture. Across the years and in places around the world, I have been blessed with the riches of faithful friends and creative companions. My gratitude to those acknowledged here, along with others I have not been able to name, above all those in Germany over recent years who have made our home a true "Heimat."

One last word of gratitude, which exceeds all others: my abiding thanks to my daughters Emma and Madeline, to whom I dedicate this volume. Beyond the precious gift of our natural bond, I am ever grateful for their deep goodness, their passionate creativity as artists, and their fidelity—each in their way—to the conviction that "another world is possible." In such things they remind me of what matters most: that the chance of home has to do with the gift of "love, with its vast geography of grace." These poems arise from memories and hopes we've gathered through the years and which have held us through it all. When the poems sing, theirs are the voices I often hear. And when they touch the sense of home that abides through the changes, theirs is the presence I so keenly feel. Their love is the mark of a promise that has come the distance and now carries on ahead.

ABOUT PARACLETE PRESS

Who We Are

As the publishing arm of the Community of Jesus, Paraclete Press presents a full expression of Christian belief and practice—from Catholic to Evangelical, from Protestant to Orthodox, reflecting the ecumenical charism of the Community and its dedication to sacred music, the fine arts, and the written word. We publish books, recordings, sheet music, and DVDs that nourish the vibrant life of the church and its people.

What We Are Doing
Books

PARACLETE PRESS BOOKS show the richness and depth of what it means to be Christian. While Benedictine spirituality is at the heart of who we are and all that we do, our books reflect the Christian experience across many cultures, time periods, and houses of worship.

We have many series, including *Paraclete Essentials; Paraclete Fiction; Paraclete Giants;* and the new *The Essentials of...*, devoted to Christian classics. Others include *Voices from the Monastery* (men and women monastics writing about living a spiritual life today), *Active Prayer,* the award-winning *Paraclete Poetry,* and new for young readers: *The Pope's Cat.* We also specialize in gift books for children on the occasions of Baptism and First Communion, as well as other important times in a child's life, and books that bring creativity and liveliness to any adult spiritual life.

The MOUNT TABOR BOOKS series focuses on the arts and literature as well as liturgical worship and spirituality; it was created in conjunction with the Mount Tabor Ecumenical Centre for Art and Spirituality in Barga, Italy.

Music

The PARACLETE RECORDINGS label represents the internationally acclaimed choir *Gloriæ Dei Cantores*, the *Gloriæ Dei Cantores Schola*, and the other instrumental artists of the *Arts Empowering Life Foundation*.

Paraclete Press is the exclusive North American distributor for the Gregorian chant recordings from St. Peter's Abbey in Solesmes, France. Paraclete also carries all of the Solesmes chant publications for Mass and the Divine Office, as well as their academic research publications.

In addition, PARACLETE PRESS SHEET MUSIC publishes the work of today's finest composers of sacred choral music, annually reviewing over 1,000 works and releasing between 40 and 60 works for both choir and organ.

Video

Our DVDs offer spiritual help, healing, and biblical guidance for a broad range of life issues including grief and loss, marriage, forgiveness, facing death, understanding suicide, bullying, addictions, Alzheimer's, and Christian formation.

Learn more about us at our website:
www.paracletepress.com or phone us
toll-free at 1.800.451.5006

 SCAN TO READ MORE

YOU MAY ALSO BE INTERESTED IN . . .

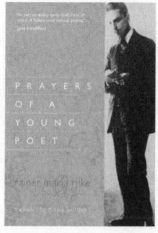

Prayers of a Young Poet
Rainer Maria Rilke

Translated by Mark S. Burrows
ISBN 978-1-61261-641-4 | $16.00 Paperback

"A Powerful alchemy of the heart."
—BILL MOYERS, journalist and political commentator

"This extraordinary early-draft form of some of Rilke's most famous poems
somehow evokes, for me, Leonardo da Vinci's notebooks—it shows the same mix
of surety, roughness, genius, and the sense of precipitous creative speed. Rilke's
poetry always reminds us what a direct pondering of intimacy and depth might
look like. I am most grateful for these muscular translations and Mark Burrows's
extended introductory comments. . . ."

—JANE HIRSHFIELD, poet and translator; author most recently of
Ten Windows: How Great Poems Transform the World

"A hauntingly beautiful book. . . . In these pages, Rilke dances in the dark to the
tune of his own poems, his reluctant partner the elusive God he woos. The effect
is irresistible: an invitation to join in the dance no reader can refuse."

—ANGELA ALAIMO O'DONNELL
poet and author of *Saint Sinatra & Other Poems*

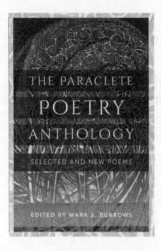

The Paraclete Poetry Anthology
Selected and New Poems

Mark S. Burrows, editor,
Foreword by Jon M. Sweeney

ISBN 978-1-612-61906-4 | $20.00 Paperback

"Consider this a short course for the soul. Or, perhaps, the syllabus to last a lifetime. . . . Gathered here we find selected and new poems from a contemplative monk or three, an Episcopal priest, a rabbi, a protege of Thomas Merton, an Iranian-German poet, a theologian, a flock of English professors, and poets from Ireland, Poland, West Virginia and Tennessee. Tucked amid the poets' roster, we find Rainer Maria Rilke, considered one of the most lyrically intense German-language poets, in new and previous translations by Burrows. . . . You'll wear out the pages and the binding before you're ever ready to put down this book."

—BARBARA MAHANY, *Chicago Tribune*

"Paraclete is a house firmly rooted in presenting and curating religious poetry as that part of the verbal experience that, being couched more deeply in the aesthetic than the didactic, has deep resonance and potent significance for the shaping of the surrounding culture itself and, as well, for the integration of individual experience into the communal, surrounding, historical, and evolving one. . . . It means the on-going giving away and sharing of God with humility through mystery."

—PHYLLIS TICKLE (1934–2015)

The anthology spans the first ten years of the poetry series at Paraclete Press. Included are poems by Phyllis Tickle, Scott Cairns, Paul Mariani, Anna Kamieńska, Fr. John-Julian, SAID, Bonnie Thurston, Greg Miller, William Woolfitt, Rami Shapiro, Thomas Lynch, Paul Quenon, and Rainer Maria Rilke.

Available through most booksellers or through Paraclete Press.
www.paracletepress.com • 1-800-451-5006
Try your local bookstore first.